To the Di Pieros of both generations

Some pray to marry the man they love,
My prayer will somewhat vary:
I humbly pray to Heaven above
That I love the man I marry.

Rose Pastor Stokes

The Art of
Staying
in Love

The Art of Staying in Love

Joseph E. Kerns

AVE MARIA PRESS
AND
TWENTY-THIRD PUBLICATIONS

The Art of Staying in Love is a co-publishing project of
Twenty-Third Publications, Fort Wayne, Indiana 46802, and
Ave Maria Press, Notre Dame, Indiana 46556.

Copyright © 1970 Twenty-Third Publications

Library of Congress Catalog Card Number: 77-144041

ISBN 0-87793-028-7

Printed in the United States of America

Contents

". . . till death do us part"

Our Problem Today

Marriage isn't a word to us American Catholics. It's a sentence. The only thing we're sure to remember the Church saying about "the holy state of matrimony" is that, once you're in it, you can't get out.

True, we've also been told it's a vocation, a call from God. But a call from God isn't a once-in-a-lifetime thing. You have to answer it every day. When you walk into a movie, and the hero and heroine are standing at the altar, you know it's the end. When you enter a church and see them there, it's the beginning. And it can be a comedy, a tragedy, or the greatest love story the world has known. They've had to answer many questions before the priest would agree to meet them there, but the questions only asked how ready they are to get married. What somebody should have inquired about is how ready they are to stay that way.

When our ancestors would swear to take each other "till death do us part," they weren't promising as much as we are. Many a bride would be burying two husbands before she reached her thirties. When St. Paul writes about the "young widows," he's thinking of teenage girls. But in this age of penicillin and heart transplants a couple will still have almost half their years of coping with each other when their youngest child is in high school.

The reaction of so many Americans to this new situation is to design marriages the way they design their clothes — one for the spring and summer years, one for the fall and winter. It looks practical, and yet we should all know better from our experience with problems like tension between the races. There's no sense thinking you can change some laws and relax if what really needs changing is some people. Putting on a wedding ring didn't make us any less ourselves. Neither will taking it off. The same problem of coping with our middle-aged selves would follow us into a second marriage. Falling in love was easy. Staying in love is our problem. If there's an art to loving, this is it.

To be loved, be lovable.

Ovid

Marriage is a thing you've got to give your whole mind to.

Henrik Ibsen

Chapter 1

The First Way

Even the first few months that follow a wedding show us the truth of John Thomas's dictum: A marriage license is only a learner's permit. At first there's emotion, ecstasy, discovery. Then the wedding presents begin to look worn and scratched. The honeymoon is forgotten. The world's two greatest lovers seem to know what each is going to do before it's done. The only discoveries now are things about each other that get on their nerves.

This is the moment of truth. For the first time they're forced to confront the fact that there's never any rest. Love either grows or dies.

13

The first anxious efforts to make it grow can end in panic. There isn't much to talk about anymore. The stories about the years before they met have all been told. All the new relatives have been commented on. The arrangements for day-to-day living with each other have all been made. They know who takes a shower first and what vegetables one of them just can't stand.

It's hard to think up greater compliments than they've already paid each other. Emotion can't be turned on hotter and hotter like water. Each of them feels a secret guilt and terror. They just can't make their love grow.

They don't have to. Love is a flower. It grows of itself. All you can ever do is take care of it. *And the first way is to love attentively.*

Marriage brings a change that has no parallel in earlier years. The experience that's human life is now to be shared with someone. This is hard, but there are four rules that make it a little easier.

The first one: *Feel the other's feelings.* This isn't something you learn in an afternoon. Two bodies need a certain amount of practice before they can be one. Two minds are even more awkward. Each of us is so used to centering on himself — worrying, providing, defending — that it takes a constant effort to pay attention to someone else. Deep down there's a fear that, if we ever stopped taking care of ourselves, nobody else would. We'd be hurt. We'd die. Day in, day out, we have to keep turning away from ourselves to this person we've married.

We have to be alert to constant changes — when she pales at the way we drive, when he begins to worry about his job. There have to be hundreds of mental notes on what this person is like, a constant discarding of first impressions. It's only to others that a human being is contradictory and inconsistent. Every twinge of emotion, every movement of his hand is obeying an inner logic. This is what we have to discover. How do things look to this woman I've married? Why does this husband do the things he does? The most common tragedy in marriage isn't pain. It's loneliness, boredom, unsatisfied longings, a slow daily death as an individual because this other individual doesn't know you, the growing drabness of a person who feels he'd be laughed at if he were himself.

But you can't feel another person's feelings till you know they're there. The first rule for attentive loving demands a second: *Spot the signals.* Of course, it takes months, even years to learn those thousand different tones of voice, those frowns and scratches and shiftings in a chair. What the one you love needs more than anything else you have to give is the time it will take to note them all. A night without TV, or even a couple of minutes together between dessert and the dishes, will teach you more than all the marriage manuals in print.

You have to notice what things impress this person who shares your life. If you like her clam chowder, it isn't enough to ask for a second helping. She loves to know why you want more. You have to keep asking what things make you hard for this other to live with — that sloppiness with toothpaste, that tendency to nag. They say that the only way Charles Laughton learned he was still being Captain Bligh at home was when his wife remarked that she'd once played The Bride of Frankenstein.

Everyone has his own private set of storm warnings. They should be learned at the earliest possible moment — his sudden silence when you reach for the phone, her pursed lips when you bite into a sandwich. Wives seem to pick them up in a month or two. For a husband, at least in the early years, the best policy is: When in doubt, stop what you're doing and kiss her.

The third rule is the hardest of all to follow. *Continue the courtship.* Try to retain the courtesies you showed this person before you proposed. You can often tell whether two people are married by watching them get into a car. If they're still single, he'll be holding the door for her. If they're not, he'll be at the wheel growling "Hurry up." If they're single, she'll diet. If they're married, she'll relax.

Every possible care should be taken to preserve the monuments to love. Certain times, for example. There are anniversaries, not just of the wedding but of the first date you had, the moment you met. Certain places in the world should be regarded as yours because you were happy there as no one had been before you — the restaurant where a certain dinner was eaten, the pavement that was strolled so many times. For couples who have to start with the cheapest apartment in town, the honk of a freight train in the night will forever be "our song."

The last rule is the easiest but the most important: *Let the other love.* In our anxiety to give, we often forget that the most noble and deeply moving gesture of love is receiving. Nobody wants to be a charity case. The one you give to also wants to give. Those clumsy fumblings and tasteless gifts are like money, faded, ugly, but standing for something precious, a person's love.

"I can take care of myself." But if you're married, sometimes you shouldn't. That care for you is the only way your partner can think of to ease the demands of love. He or she can get affectionate at some ridiculous times, but love, like gold, is where you find it. Remembering to say thanks, learning, when you're tired or sick or in a hurry, to decline with obvious regret, is one of the most important things in marriage. We're told that it's more blessed to give than to receive. But there's a way of receiving that's really giving, and it can make two people happier than they've ever been in their lives.

There are other ways of staying in love, but they all begin with this one: Love attentively. Feel her feelings. Spot his signals. Continue the courtship. Let each other love.

If you do, love will grow of itself. What started it was the discovery of this person. What will keep it alive are constant discoveries that you haven't really known her or him. Anxious spouses are always asking, "What can I do for you?" To one who loves them the answer is simple, "Just be and be here."

Chapter 2

A Second Way

Love may be blind, but a month or two of marriage opens its eyes. The dream girl emerges as a nightmare. The Prince Charming who proposed on bended knee turns out not to be a prince — and not to be very charming.

To remain not simply married but happy about their condition, a husband and wife have to realize that the most corrosive poison in the world is wishful thinking. The only one each of them is married to is the other, and if the first way to stay in love is to love this person attentively, the second is: *Love this person as she or he is.*

They have to keep reminding themselves

of three facts so obvious that they're always overlooked. The first: *This person isn't you.*

"The two shall be one — and I'm the one." That delusion obsesses every bride and groom. We expect this person we've married to be normal — in other words, like us. We're annoyed to discover that women don't like keeping still and watching a football game, that men don't thrill at the prospect of dressing for a party.

A husband can explode into profanities about a woman's fears. A wife can find it hard to admire anyone who's sloppy at table. A genuine pity for someone incapable of enjoying a concert isn't love. In fact, like anger and contempt, it can destroy love.

Yet, you can't save a marriage by keeping your eyes shut. The only thing you can do is learn to appreciate the otherness of this other, to notice how it's the very thing that makes marriage so rich and full a way to live. You do things you'd never have done yourself. You see places you'd never have gone to. You meet and find yourself actually enjoying people you'd never have known.

The strange proof of how badly all of us want this enrichment is the way we're annoyed when the other is like ourselves.

This husband can be just as afraid of people as you are. This wife can have just as bad a habit of talking about herself. Instead of a wonderful other, you find your own ugly self right in front of you. You see what your family has had to put up with for so many years.

This other isn't you. A second fact is even harder to realize. This other isn't simply "the opposite sex," a new improved model of one of our parents. A certain resemblance to that father whose fondled little girl you were is probably the thing about this person that made you glow the day he noticed you and invited you out. But he doesn't like to grow flowers the way your father did. He thinks it's silly. This woman doesn't know how to make pancakes. "I'm my father. Why isn't she my mother?" It isn't always a happy thing to discover that females aren't alike.

There's no reincarnation. Our parents have only lived once. If we realize this but still don't enjoy this different person, it may be because we've never really seen her or him. All we've seen is a "woman" or a "man" — a breed about which our own sex has a folklore that it handed on to us. The world is swarming with unlicensed experts on how to cope with the other half of the race. So are divorce courts. As the proverb warns, there are three types of woman no man understands: old ones, middle-aged ones and young ones.

"I know what you meant by that word."

"I'll tell you why you really cried."

Wouldn't it be hard to stay in love with the drab uncomplicated person we'd be able to understand?

This other isn't yourself. This other isn't "the opposite sex." In fact, this other isn't even the way she or he used to be. We see that all too plainly at times. But do we understand it? A woman who's spent all day coping with children just can't love you the way a bride can. But aren't they your children? If she's tired and faded, isn't it from all the whooping cough and clogged drains and summonses by teachers that the two of you have been through?

You can't be blamed for wanting your husband always to be the man you remember from that storybook honeymoon. But the happiness of those days can still be yours.

Come, grow old with me.
The best is yet to be.

Isn't that balding cough-prone figure who's resulted from an anxiety to provide the things he's wanted for his wife more precious to you than any bridegroom? Love can make the two of you the only two in the world who aren't afraid of time.

The engineer at a radio station can do awesome things with his dials. If he's new, he'll make every voice into the same ideal sound. If he's a veteran, he'll make each of them itself, unique among voices. The same is true of people who marry. Loving the other as she or he is doesn't mean just shutting your eyes and letting things happen. It means working for this person. She or he needs help and was hoping to find it in marriage. But the work isn't an effort to fashion the model human being. It's to help a very special human being to be his or her truest self.

Let this person talk. Create the assurance that any idea, any suggestion, any feeling can be expressed without fear or embarrassment.

Let her or him do a couple of things alone. We can never sing along with certain people. We'd spoil the music. Love would be better served by calling the world's attention to this wealth of theirs that we can never share. A husband can brag about the books his wife reads. She can have him tell their guests about his job.

Let him be with the boys some nights.

Let her have her bridge club. It's better than going out together for something neither of you will enjoy.

Finally, if this unique human being has to be corrected, let it be only for the hypocrisy that keeps her from being herself, the sloth that allows him to settle for less than what he wants. We should ask ourselves frankly what that impulse is that makes us want to redesign a person. It isn't love. It's often the desire to make this other be what we'll never be ourselves. The wife who keeps saying No to God will bore her husband with sermons. The husband who doesn't know what real unselfishness is will keep a harried woman moving toward a mirage.

Doubting ourselves, we want a sense of achievement. We forget that human beings can never be shaped. They can only be loved. This is why a marriage is lived in mystery. You give and never see the real results.

This is good for us. It keeps us honest. We'll never try to catch the world's attention if we're not sure what we'll have to show.

What God confided to us on that wedding day wasn't just a spouse. It was a person. And like the kingdom of God that

Christ described in parables, a person is a jumble of wheat and weeds. That vocation of ours was a call to love this attractive, exasperating creature. He does, and he isn't sentimental. If he loves, it's because he sees something that deserves love, and if you could only know this person as he does, you'd see it too. The most constant prayer of a husband and wife should be to appreciate each other.

The climate that makes love grow isn't fantasy. It's truth. The person you've actually married will be far more wonderful than the one you've dreamed about. Even when that feeling comes that you just can't live with her, you'll know you could never live without her.

Love that's wise
Will not say all it means.

Edwin A. Robinson

Chapter 3

The Best Way

It's a wise groom who has to be dragged to the altar. He knows what love is.

It's death. You still get up in the morning. You still work and talk. Yet there isn't anymore you. These things are being done for someone else.

Whether we'd fall in love depended once on that someone else — what she looked like, how considerate he was. Whether we stay in love depends on ourselves. It can't be synthesized in a laboratory. It only grows in nature. Once it sprouts, the thing that decides how strong it will grow isn't what we receive. It's what we give. Both the first way to keep it growing, "Love this person attentively," and the second, "Love this person as she is," depend on a third way, *"Love this person more than you love yourself."*

That means, entrust yourself. When a human being exposes his body, he exposes himself. But really to expose ourselves takes longer than a wedding night. Letting another person see you as you are means giving him the power to hurt you, and we've all spent years on disguises to keep anybody from doing that. The bored sigh and laugh-on-demand have to be taken off. We have to reveal those fears we have — of the dark, a doctor's needle, having children. We have to disclose those secret desires. They aren't really silly. Something in us that we don't really know has certain needs. But the smaller they are, the harder it is to talk about them. It's like going to the dentist. No matter how much good it will do us, we dread it every time.

Experience will make it a little more possible. We'll remember what it was like the last time — that relief at being known, that awareness, worth all the pain of exposure, that this person who sees us isn't turning away. We're actually lovable.

It's strange the way newlyweds look at time. It represents life itself, so they keep it — not big chunks but little pieces that they won't even give the one they've married. There are moments they've always put aside for certain things, a game that has to be watched, a shopping trip that simply has to be made. These moments have always been theirs. They're the truest most independent life they've had. If even these few moments disappear, it seems that they will too.

Yet this is what has to happen. To fall in love may have only taken one or two seconds. To stay in love takes every second you have. You have to be willing to share them down to the last one, to let someone else decide how even that one will be spent, to entrust yourself.

Adapt yourself. Love is an exercise in frustration. The question we awaken with every morning, "What would I like today?" has to be changed to "What would this person like?"

Singers are born great. Nurses acquire greatness. Married people have it thrust upon them. To be married is to leave the window up when you want it down, to watch someone else's favorite program, to kiss when you have a headache, to turn the music down, to watch your language, to be patient without sighing or sulking or taking yourself too seriously.

It's a call to entrust yourself, adapt yourself, bestir yourself. Love is something you work at. It isn't always possible to feel emotion, but it is always possible to do good. Of course, we human beings are magnetized toward comfort. Once we have that, we stop. It takes longer than a honeymoon to train ourselves to keep moving, to bring happiness when it hasn't even been asked for.

But it doesn't take much money or even time. There are gestures, trivial in themselves but amazing in what they do — a squeeze, a smile, a snack together. There are permanent rituals of love, the way a coat is held, a tone of voice, certain titles of affection — not Snookums, perhaps, but at least Dear.

Marriage, in other words, is a call from Christ to sacrifice ourselves. When we hear the gospel say that we have to follow him even to the cross, we imagine ourselves being stood against a wall. It could come to that if some people in the world had their way, but for nine Christians out of ten, the crucifixion is giving in to the one they've married. The oldest equation in mathematics is $h + w = c$: Husband plus Wife equals Conflict. And just as in war, it's death to lose.

But there's a peculiar thing about marriage conflicts. Victory is always a defeat, and defeat can always be victory.

A remark is made. The perfect answer comes to mind. If this has ever happened before and you've dropped your H-bomb, remember the look on the target's face. Was it worth it?

Sometimes the other is clearly in the wrong. You can punish, humiliate, demand apologies and get them. But what good will it do? You'll feel ashamed. And you may never be loved again.

"It's not fair!"

That's right. It's not fair. But take your choice. Do you want justice or do you want this person you've married? Sometimes you can't have both.

This is why lovers never say, "Do this or else." A person who loses face can never have the same feeling for the one who caused such an experience.

Even the liturgy seems afraid to tell brides and grooms the exasperating thing about marriage. Never will you have your way again. Even if you could, you wouldn't want it. You can't be happy anymore if this other person isn't. The sooner you admit this to yourself, the better off you'll be. No matter who wins the argument, you lose. Victory is always a defeat.

The trick is to change your tactics. Take advantage of the fact that defeat can always be victory. You'll want a Volkswagen. She'll want a Cadillac. Compromise on a Chevrolet. You'll have her love and your self-respect.

Of course, some negotiations aren't easy. After supper a husband feels like staying home. He's been out all day. A wife feels like going out. She's been home all day. There's no compromise between in and out.

The sooner they frankly admit that they need each other and that this is more important than anything else, the sooner they'll see what they should do. Of course, making this admission won't be easy. Their words of love for each other have always come of themselves like children rushing to greet a favorite uncle. This time the children are being thrust forward and told to do what's proper. They have to be dealt with firmly. They can hesitate and mumble, but the idea has to come across, "I want you more than I want myself."

No two people can hurt each other like a husband and wife. Words are said that the tongue would give anything to take back. But it's too late.

The victim turns away. The attacker just stands there.

The thing to beware of at such a horrible moment is the chasm that can open between two people who don't know what to do, the Great Silence. Once it opens, it begins to widen. The longer they wait, the harder it is to cross, till each of them finds himself alone. No matter how ridiculous you feel, say something. Do something. Grab each other and don't let go till one of you can talk.

Be willing to make the first move. Human problems can never be solved by justice, only by love. It's maddening to realize this, and yet deep down don't we already know that love is better than justice? It's the most precious thing you have.

This is Good Friday, to love this person more than you love yourself. But Good Friday is always followed by Easter. There's no more wonderful experience in life than looking at a special face, seeing its happiness, and knowing you're the one who caused it.

Love is a stairway. A husband and wife can stay on one level as long as they live if they want to. But each time one of them loves the other more than he loves himself, they'll be startled to find themselves on a higher level. They thought they knew what it was like to be in love. Now they see they were only children. It's different and far more wonderful than they ever dreamed. A few years of climbing that stairway will show them why people like Viktor Frankl claim they never envy those who are young. "All they have are hopes. I have memories."

We must cultivate our garden.

Voltaire

Chapter 4

The Climate for Love

Not so many years ago a lady in West Virginia decided that the best thing she could do for a nearby college would be to improve its campus. The college soon discovered that it had just been endowed with a dozen cedars of Lebanon.

Never have 12 sprigs a couple of inches high received such attention. The Republic of Lebanon, the government of the United States, the trustees, the president, the director of buildings and grounds, the maintenance foreman, not to mention the Department of Agriculture, which sent an agent every month, were giving directions to the gardener.

The ground was raked and fertilized. Of course, three feet below the surface there was a seam of coal. The treelets were watched and measured and shielded by a wire fence, but were also buried in more snow than Lebanon ever sees. By the end of a typical August when the West Virginia clay cracks open and any grass that isn't burnt to death is a tough brown wire, the cedars of Lebanon were pronounced dead. The government agent made it official.

This is the story of more than one love that has taken root in our country. It's died, and people have blamed the man and woman who were supposed to take care of it. But whether it would survive and grow didn't only depend on them. A marriage that would thrive in the Fijis might not last a year on islands like Manhattan, Staten or Long. Our cultural climate will only tolerate a certain kind of love. It has to be able to survive two peculiarities of this country.

The first is status. A man's is determined by his work, a woman's by her husband's work. To the neighbors she'll be the barber's wife. If you don't think American couples care about this, notice the titles they've devised for a janitor.

The most highly esteemed work of all is

making money. This is why those who aren't sure how much prestige their job will bring try to look as rich as their neighbors. But this is hard on love. A wife may always be tired when her husband comes home, annoyed at everything, bored for lack of children, because when they settled down after the honeymoon, they didn't live on his salary and put hers in the bank. They used both of them to create a style of life that they can't give up.

The people these lackadaisical Americans need the most aren't always the ones they pay the most. A city detective doesn't make nearly as much as the girl on a lipstick commercial. Instead of being proud of her husband who's doing so much good, more than one American wife feels annoyed with him as they leave the home of one of her friends from college.

Yet status isn't nearly as hard on love as another oddity of this cultural climate, separation. In the Philippines a couple are expected to spend their first year with the husband's parents. Aunts, brothers, in-laws, outlaws — dozens of people ply the girl with bracelets and recipes and counsel. They say it isn't good for her to be alone.

Americans disagree. She and her inexperienced husband may be hundreds of miles from either family. They don't know anybody on their street, even in their apartment building. A normal human appetite for companionship has to be satisfield by a single person. The happiness that has to linger through an entire day is what this partner provided from suppertime last night till they fell asleep.

Neither of them has had any experience that would prepare them for this. The girl has always come from work to familiar faces in a familiar scene. The onrush of young love makes anything possible for a couple of months. There will soon be friends. But what happens if these people also have to be left, and then another set, as the company keeps awarding promotions to another city?

The man has had to talk to people in his college dorm. But they weren't women. True, he's been alone with a girl on dates, but he could tell her the same jokes he'd told the last one. Even when there was only this one, a date can only last so many hours.

The first things a couple have to find if they're to survive in these United States are three or four things they both like to do. Movies, Chinese food, bowling, window shopping — they have to sample everything, and they have to notice whether the other is really enjoying this or just being helpful.

Things that were the other's idea have to be listed in three columns: 1) What I like; 2) What I don't mind because she or he likes it so much; 3) What I'm sorry but I just can't stand. The longer the first two columns grow, the easier it will be to stay in love.

Since most emotional outlets have been blocked by an American's need to smile in public, every moment you spend with the person you've married carries a heavy charge. Not only is there no one else to love. There's no one to swear with or cry to. If even this partner isn't an outlet, something in love will die. In the United States it isn't even enough to learn what the other's emotional needs really are. You have to show that you respect them.

This is why American quarrels are not only more sudden but more alarming. If this one last person turns away, you'll be alone. Americans have to be more careful than others to let the past be past. They have each other. They love each other. This is more important than what's happened between them.

The separation their love has to adapt to isn't just from relatives and old neighbors. It's from each other. The solitary wife is as American as the hot dog. A baby is fascinating like no one else in the world, but it isn't much for conversation. Even when it does begin to have an idea or two, they make you send it to school.

American husbands are no better than other ones as talkers (which means they're pretty bad). Their idea of companionship is to watch the superbowl together. They don't realize the pressures that build up in a woman. Forty-eight hours is the longest she can wait. Then he simply has to hear about the neighbors. One husband was awakened at what he noticed was 2 a.m. It wasn't a burglar or even one of the children, just his wife saying, "Talk to me!"

The price of good talk is sacrifice. An American husband doesn't have to bring flowers home, but he shouldn't come in without some news of the world. She can get the wars and stock quotations from David Brinkley. What she wants from the man who loves her is news about people. It's a nuisance to have to notice them, but there are few wiser things he can do.

He'll find there are some whose very name will get her talking. Like a newspaper editor he should always have a feature ready on one of these for evenings when there's nothing to report. I know a man whose wife has never forgiven Pope Paul for the English Mass. When nothing else comes to mind, he makes a remark about the language God enjoys. It never fails. Rage and eloquence leave her pleasantly exhausted by bedtime.

Trying to vary the evening routine is also a sacrifice. It calls for as much ingenuity as was needed during the courtship months when they were seeing each other almost every day. A dinner date is ideal, but she demands as little as she did during courtship. She's never lost the thrill of going out, even for ice cream.

In this land of office buildings a man can spend most of his waking hours with a woman he isn't married to. She's more attractive and personable than most. That's why the company has promoted her. She always looks her best. She listens but doesn't have to be listened to. He's never seen her crying. No matter how alarmed she'd be at threatening anybody's marriage, he can't help comparing his wife to her.

After hours of coping with children and gadgets that never work, a woman is tired — too tired to dress up. But if she would dress up, she wouldn't feel so tired. Nor would her husband when he saw her.

With a little imagination he himself can

add to this moment. An occasional scarf or pin will help her to keep those dresses from looking familiar. A moment's trouble to tell her how she looks will ease her anxiety over what babies and time have done to her. In fact, it will give her the finishing touch, that glow of a woman who knows she's loved.

American business, that leaves a couple to eat and sleep without each other, can make them citizens of two distant countries, Work and Children. There's a trade in goods and services, a nonaggression pact, but little interest in each other's homeland. Husbands are usually blamed for this. Wives should blame themselves. A conversation isn't just a set of polite inquiries. It's an exchange of fears and problems and plans.

What a husband has to understand is the monotony of life in her country. The girl who got A's in sociology is rubbing fingerprints from walls. The bride who glowed as she took her first roast from the oven is pushing herself through chores that people seem to think will do themselves. The mother who could cope with three boys finds herself strong and well and useless now that they're married.

But the climate that can be so harsh is really one of the best in the world for love.

In West Africa two people marry because a man with six goats was looking for a wife and a man with a daughter was looking for goats. In the United States they marry because they like each other. Love demands equality, and American wives are more equal than husbands. What love will be depends on what two people dream it can be. In this country they dream it can be wonderful. With grandparents who crossed an ocean and astronauts who've reached the moon, they're very serious about their dreams.

A compliment is something like a kiss through a veil.

Victor Hugo

Chapter 5

Growing Pains

When the climate is right, a couple are taking expert care of their love, and it's beginning to grow, they aren't always on a cloud. We crazy human beings want to be loved and yet don't want to. We blush and squirm. To be told how wonderful we are is a thrill and a torture. Any two of us whose life is a constant exchange of love have to learn the truth about praise.

It isn't forbidden fruit. It's like love: beautiful when it's given, wonderful when it's received, only evil and harmful if it's demanded.

The most reliable sign of a truly great man or woman is an alertness to good in others. This doesn't mean they flatter you. As Henry Rago once noted, flattery isn't praise. It's the use of praise. Praise is what comes out before we realize what we're saying. It isn't trying to do anything. It's just acknowledging what we see.

Once it's a habit, it can make us feel like Adam on his first day. We've been so engrossed in ourselves that we've never seen the world we live in. It's amazing to find how much more often we ourselves are praised. Apparently we're more attractive. Praise is beautiful when it's given.

And so wonderful when it's received. This event that a mysterious providence keeps bringing into our lives is a reminder. "You weren't made for God's glory. You are that glory, a radiance that shows he's present. You aren't here just to benefit the world, and yet he does intend to let you share his power to bring it good. One impulse that will turn it to good will be its reaction to you." A husband will arrive in heaven because of the wife he was so in love with. A boy will do great things to be like his father.

By loving me You have made me lovable.

Augustine is describing each of us as well as himself. When this person you've married gets a glimpse of you as you are, she won't be able to help herself. You'll be praised.

It will feel so good that you'll find yourself worrying whether you do things just to have more of this pleasure. It might be wise to consult the people who've had the most experience of this particular problem, the saints. Francis de Sales, who sometimes had to hide from the crowds who revered him, told a friend,

> Left to myself I would be tempted to make a fool of myself to undeceive these people. But we have to live with Christian sincerity, playing neither the fool nor the wise man.

To a married woman who was afraid that, if she talked about religion, it would look as though she were a saint, he wrote,

> Never do or say anything to win praise. Never leave anything undone or unsaid for fear of being praised . . . I no more believe I am perfect because I talk about perfection than I'd believe myself Italian because I speak Italian.

Singing and piano playing are meant to be listened to. If a wife who can give her husband these pleasures is pushed and pulled by conflicting desires, she should listen to Teresa of Avila.

What would become of us if each of us hid all the little wit she possessed? Nobody has that much. Let each of us bring out whatever she has in her with all humility to cheer the others up.

People like Ignatius Loyola and Bernard of Clairvaux would agree. After debates with themselves they seem to have come to the same conclusion: If a thing is good, say it or do it.

When you're praised for it, you're being given a reminder. You happen to be loved. By trying to ignore your discomfort and accept the praise you'll acknowledge how much you need this reminder.

True, when your husband praises you, he's praising the one who made you all you are. That God is coming into his life through you, and you don't want to be a distraction. But this doesn't mean you have to bore him now with a sermon. What it does mean was illustrated for me one night by a couple and their little girl.

We were at dinner, and in the midst of the table talk the girl cried, "Mother! You're so beautiful!" Before anybody could think of what to say, her mother smiled at her and told her a Russian folk tale.

It seems that a little girl was lost one time in a very large city. She didn't know where she lived and couldn't even tell the police her name. She just kept saying that her mother was the most beautiful woman in the world. They didn't seem to find this much of a clue, but a few hours later a peasant woman with stringy hair and coarse wrinkled skin came into the station. The little girl cried, "Mother!"

To react like this to a compliment requires a larger assortment of Russian folk tales than most of us have on hand. Still, the principle is a good one: The proper response to praise is praise. Find something you can sincerely compliment in this person who has complimented you. At least turn the conversation to him.

Not as though you were warding off evil. It's just an attempt to be honest. By bringing a pleasurable moment to a close you're acknowledging that you didn't make yourself. You still have the memory of this time when you've been praised. Praise is so wonderful when it's received.

It's only evil and harmful if it's demanded. It has to come of itself. Forcing it would put us in danger of blindness, a blindness to the good in other people, a blindness to ourselves, as though there were nothing in us that would awaken praise.

This is why Christ has urged us to be "poor in spirit." We're to deal with people as we would if we didn't have our gifts. Beauty, talent, whatever we've received from God should be treasured and used but not paraded. The knowledge of how little we had to do with it should incline us to be simple and artless. If people regard us as a character, it should happen despite our efforts, not because of them.

Anne Lindbergh once remarked,

The most exhausting thing in life, I have discovered, is being insincere. That is why so much of social life is exhausting; one is wearing a mask. *(Gift from the Sea)*

The human brain is really ingenious at designing a mask that will keep all conversation on our assets. Some men don't just spend their money. They present themselves as "the Success," name dropping, deal describing, investment counseling. Some women, instead of doing things they like and avoiding what they don't like, prefer to suffer in society's latest mask. They'll get a Scotch down if it chokes them. One who'd given her maid the privilege of sampling an hors d'oeuvre she'd devised for a party, was told, "Well, Ma'am, everybody has their own tastes, I guess." Then as she glowered, "But it sure does taste expensive."

"The Teacher" has to show her students how little their parents know. "The Expert" is forever correcting laymen. But few human beings are more exasperating, and more pathetic, than those who wear a mask at home.

One is "a Man." He has to be waited on and lets things stay where they fall. Every now and then he overturns everybody's plans as a reminder of who's in charge. If his wife insists on speaking once in a while or begins to cry, he goes into his tolerant routine. "Women can't help their absurdities." Of course, when he's depressed, the house is a funeral parlor.

Many a real man has to cope with a partner in a Woman mask. She alone knows the secrets of marriage. He can manage an office, it seems, but once he opens the door to that living room, every step is a blunder.

When he tells the children what to do, he finds they've been warned. If he tries to show love, he's made to feel clumsy.

One of the most practical ways to acknowledge the God who made us is to stay away from masks. We want people's attention to be where it ought to be. If praise comes, it will have to come of itself.

It will. And it will be different now. When you wore a mask, even the person you married never saw you. It was the Executive or the Sophisticate who was constantly calling for attention, not you. Now she or he will make you realize how wonderful it is to be yourself.

The reason we don't love more is that we think we already love enough.

Joseph E. Kerns

Chapter 6

Success Is Failure

Imperfect love holds a danger for us. We're sometimes content to have nothing more.

This remark by a shrewd observer of life, Francis de Sales, explains so much of the boredom in marriage. Love has no stability. It's either growing or dying. But once it's beyond the early stage it can grow a little and die a little every month and begin to look drab. Just because a couple aren't filing for divorce, this doesn't make them the world's champion lovers. If they drift along for years without seeing more in each other, it may be because of an attitude

Lincoln Steffens used to complain about in his attempts to clean up city governments.

> The regular members of the Christian churches, thinking they have Christianity, can no more get to it than the righteous, thinking they are good, can be made good — for anything. Christianity will not work with Christians.
>
> But, as Jesus learned by hard experience and taught so clearly, Christianity does work with sinners.

The reason we don't love more is that we think we already love enough. More than one dull marriage is dull because the people in it are spending their days thanking God that they're not like other couples.

The God who has been revealed by Christ is always tense, always looking for an excuse to give us something. One thing, and one thing only, holds him back. He doesn't want to hurt us. This is what his favors would do if we didn't realize they were favors. They'd keep us in a dream-world. So the proud man and woman are resisted.

To him we're everything. All that we do is important. But we didn't make ourselves.

54

We're nothing. We have to look at both these truths if we want to see ourselves and our spouse and our love for each other as they are.

The way to do it is best described by a phrase in John's first Epistle: "practicing the truth." We'll be more likely to see ourselves as we are if we do things that express what we are.

We can make ourselves accept the reminders that married life presents us with. For example, our public faults. More than one husband would find it easier to confess a mortal sin than to live with the fact that two close friends and his teenage daughter saw the tantrum in which he reduced his wife to tears. "Practicing the truth" consists in making ourselves apologize and forget. Sometimes we shouldn't even apologize. It would renew the other's pain by bringing the scene to life again. But we should forget.

A second reminder comes even more often, our mistakes. What we affirmed so confidently at the dinner table wasn't morally wrong. Just wrong. In one of his letters Thomas More suggests how this discovery can be an occasion for "practicing the truth."

Nothing is more sad than that men should form varying judgments about identical problems. But nothing is more rare than that after they have published their views, argued strongly for them and defended them against attack, they then, acknowledging the truth, should change their course, and as if their voyage had been in vain, sail back into the harbor they had left.

It will never be easy to repeat Mayor LaGuardia's boast, "When I make a mistake, it's a beaut." A husband or wife will fear, and not without reason, that this would just be giving the other a weapon that will be hurled back in the next engagement. But when we have genuine claims to respect, why rely on a fantasy? A frank admission to ourselves and our spouse that we were wrong will keep us aware of how things are. We're everything, and we're nothing.

These bitter moments can be sweetened by a second way of "practicing the truth": Notice the humor in your life.

What does a Christian laugh at? Not at somebody's pain. He regards mockery as a sin. Not at the grim absurdity of life. He knows it has meaning. When he laughs at Charlie Brown's entanglements with a kite, he's laughing at himself. Secure in his dignity, since he knows what he means to God, he's freely admitting that he's nothing. The world ignores him and lets its wet paint stick to the seat of his pants.

We never have to try to be clowns. Truth is funnier than fiction. Married life itself presents us with such crazy mirrors to see ourselves. The reason we've been ready to go out so much earlier than this wife we've just sermonized is that we've forgotten to shave.

"Practicing the truth" consists in accepting moments like this. It's easier than giving up things for Lent. All you do is laugh.

We can train ourselves to deal with the family in ways that acknowledge what we and they are. It's the third and probably most helpful method of practicing the truth. Often it's simply a matter of showing respect for certain things of theirs. For example, their time. If we talk to them, we can notice whether they're interested in the parade of our thoughts. We can make it easy for them to turn to something else if they want to.

A more important thing to respect is their privacy. We can be careful not to thrust ourselves into their presence whether they like it or not. Even in a sharing as complete as that of husband and wife, there are times when each should be left alone. And children have these rights as well as parents.

Finally, there can be respect for the mystery of a person. No one but God has the evidence it would take to understand everything he does. We can train ourselves to banish reflections like, "There! See how stubborn women are?" Scripture asks us,

> Who are you to judge another's servant? To his own lord he stands or falls. But he will stand, for God is able to make him stand.

This doesn't mean we can never laugh at the person we've married. Sometimes we'd be laughing at ourselves. Dr. Robert Saint-Cyr used to come regularly to treat Bernadette Soubirous. One of the nurses reports that

> Bernadette used to entertain us with imitations of him. They made us laugh so much that tears came to our eyes.

But if we want to practice the truth, we have to give ourselves a rule for laughing:

only joke about people who know you respect them.

We'd do well to cultivate certain ways of speaking. We can make ourselves be scrupulously courteous to those who depend on our approval — a husband, a child. This doesn't mean kneeling down in their presence. It can be as simple as asking instead of telling them to do things.

A new neighbor, a wife who's overdrawn the checking account, a born lip-biter will be uncomfortable in our presence. Practicing the truth consists in putting them at ease, resisting that tendency to be more stern when we see we're dealing with weakness.

It also consists in never teasing people who can't reply. Some men are comedians as soon as company arrives. They'd be furious if their wives put them through the same routine before the same audience.

There are times when another person should be allowed to star. A wife's joke doesn't have to be topped. Verbal wrestling matches sound like enjoyable conversation, but they never are. Two college graduates often circle around slowly with vague remarks, careful not to be caught unacquainted with an author. Then in a flash one of them pins the other with a title he hasn't heard of. It's declared the definitive work on the subject.

These aren't the only occasions when we practice the truth by keeping quiet. An honest examination will show that we interrupt our wife without a qualm but are cautious with other women. We can refrain from correcting people in public. To speak when the children will see how impractical their mother is may hurt them as well as reinforcing our delusion of being superior to her. As a rule, not even a child should be rebuked in the presence of others. In fact, it's an acknowledgment of his dignity to see that no aunt or grandfather or sister reminds him of misdemeanors for which he has already been punished.

The reason behind all these different methods of practicing the truth is the same. A way of speaking to people and acting toward them soon engenders a way of thinking about them. Experience keeps offering new insights into that mystery of being everything and nothing. The longer we live, the more justified will our courtesy and deference to this person who shares our life prove to be.

Chapter 7

Love consists in this, that two solitudes protect and touch and greet each other.

Rainer Maria Rilke

The Greatest Help There Is

How do people in love spend most of their time? Doing things for each other? No. Doing things together for someone else.

This is a surprise to them when they notice it. But as time goes on they see it's the best thing that could happen to them. Love is a plant. You can't make it grow. You can only remove the things that keep it from growing. In all the talk about ways of staying in love, the best remark is that of one woman, "Love is what you've been through together."

Life itself confronts you with three great experiences. If both of you pay attention to them and both get involved, you'll see that God has a way of making you stay in love.

The first is the work you have to do. A woman who loves a man becomes that man. If he learns to talk to her about his work, to confess how much it means to him and how many things he's afraid will stop him from being what he'd like to be some-day, he'll be amazed at the change in her. As one wife put it, "We're going to be a lawyer."

The work is good because it's his work. When pages of it have to be typed, she for-gets about time. When it fails, she's the one who cries. If the boss or a customer hurts him, he can still live with them. She can't. As time goes on, he may be willing to see himself in the number-two or the number-ten spot. She'll never settle for that.

It will look as though she just wants a bigger check to spend. The most humbling moment in his life will be when he sees what the real reason is. That crazy idea of how good he is, how many things he can do, how much the world should appreciate him will make him take her and love her as he never has before.

Her own distinctive work as a woman will have the same effect. This is hard to see at first, but it's clear from the moment she's pregnant. Their attention turns from themselves to someone else. Year in, year out, every decision — what to buy, where to live, how to spend a weekend — is made with an eye to the children.

From the young sophisticate who looks at her with awe to the new father who rushes into the room to kiss her to the 50-year-old who marvels at the way she stays awake till the last one is in for the night, the man she married finds her always more wonderful. Laughing together at children, cleaning up their mess, checking homework, beaming at a commencement can make love too obvious to question anymore.

The second way that life itself unites a man and woman is by the bond of pain or pleasure. The poverty of newlyweds who laugh at their furniture, a nagging sickness, sudden news of death in one of the families make the days before seem a time when they were distant from each other compared to now.

"Music I heard with you was more than music."

All those evenings on the town, all the good news he's brought home, all that awesome new pleasure they've given each other since the wedding night can deepen love if they're remembered. The house they shopped for and chose together and furnished and repaired can make them take each other's hand as they view it.

Not that they fondle each experience. No matter what good pain can do, they want it to end. When they take in a movie, it isn't because they want to stay in love. It's because they think they'll like it.

Those two hours of watching an actor is like a third experience that life provides. It's the one that made them serious about each other in the first place.

Each of them had a personal view of Christ. Formed over the years of discovering how to get along in this world, charged with deep wordless cravings, memories of guilt and forgiveness, of prayers for so many things, permeated with the longing of every bone and fibre to reach an ideal, it was something no one would understand. Other people's experiences seemed so different. And besides, even the thought of revealing them brought a chill.

Then they met. They felt an interest in each other because she looked so good and he had such a way of making you laugh. They fell in love because, without a word, each discovered that there was someone else who had a life with Christ. It was such a relief to be understood. You could relax.

64

You could talk about yourself. It was fascinating to see how differently this girl responded to him. This man who pretended to be so matter-of-fact was lovable as he'd never been before. One day, just as at the movies, they joined hands and began to watch him together.

St. Paul's words about the married man who's "divided" are being misunderstood if we think that staying absorbed in Christ would keep two people turned away from each other. It's just the opposite. Their life with him is what makes them understand each other. The wonderful destiny they share is what joins them. When she sees him trying to be a Christian, she knows what it's like. As he watches her respond in that artless way of hers to demands whose cost he knows, he wants to do so much for her.

When they deal with the Lord, they aren't thinking about their love. It would be wrong to use God as a mere means of loving someone. But nothing in their lives has a greater effect on it than being able to look at each other and echo Tertullian: "My dearest fellow-slave of Christ."

Not that they really need to talk about it. The other knows. Still, the feeling for Christ is happier and unites them more if they can express it. Praying together at night would help, if the prayers are brief and partly at least in their own words. There should be a silent part where each can speak for himself and a part where the husband speaks for the two of them.

The arrival of children means that somebody will always have to be in the house on Sunday. But the experience of joining in the same liturgy once again will show that it might be worth the trouble and expense to get a baby-sitter once a month. And the advantage of taking one day a year for some kind of praying and taking stock is that otherwise you can live with a person who feels as you do and yet never be able to talk about it.

Two persons joined to Him are joined to each other.

Joseph E. Kerns

Chapter 8

The Silent Partner

There are some days in our lives so big that it takes us years to realize what happened on them. One of them is a wedding day. There are some events so holy, so filled with God, that all we can do is accept them simply and quietly like children. One of them is a marriage. There are some gifts of God so rich and amazing and wonderful that we can't appreciate them. We have to be told and reminded of what they are. One of them is the sacrament that's made us husband and wife.

It's a shame if we were misled by all the wedding prayers. They weren't the real event. They were just to help us realize what was happening. When we deal with God we tend to expect thunder and lightning. But his work, no matter what amazing things it does to us, is so simple, so ordinary.

Take the large consecrated host that you'd find if you opened a tabernacle door. The liturgy at which it was consecrated has been over for quite some time. Yet it's still a sacrament. As long as it lasts it will be holy and can make us holy. But look at it. There's no light coming from it. To the eye it's just a piece of bread.

The same is true of your marriage. It didn't end with the ceremony that morning. Year after year, as long as you both are alive, there will be a sacrament, a visible sign that's holy and makes you holy. But like the host in the tabernacle it will look so plain, so ordinary. There won't be candles or incense. There won't be elegant hymns. That sacrament is your work, your joy in each other. That sacrament is you.

Your growth in holiness isn't going to depend on how often you'll be free to visit a church. The church where you find Christ now is your home. The charity that measures your growth is your concern for the person you've married. Whatever you do for that person Christ regards as done for him. The job you've taken to support your

wife, the meals you cook for your husband
. . . they're the sacrament, the living symbol
of how Christ and the Church are always
doing things for each other. The sacrament
is your work.

You've always known in a theoretical
way that you're loved by Christ. Now you
can see what that means by the token of .
love he's given you: a person, someone to
share your thoughts, listen to your troubles,
a person who enjoys just being with you.
You've seen time and time again that this is
your greatest happiness, just having each
other, seeing how much you mean to each
other, how new and wonderful life can be
when it's shared. This is the sacrament, the
living symbol that tells the world how Christ
and the Church enjoy each other's company,
how men speak familiarly now to a God
who became a man himself and lived
among them. The sacrament is your joy in
each other.

Marriage isn't like other sacraments.
There's no water, no chrism. To be husband
and wife it's enough to nod or take each
other's hand. Why? Because God's grace
for this person you've stood beside is simply
you. Watching you is a day-in-day-out
inspiration to your husband. Having you as
a husband is having strength when she's

69

weak, courage when she's afraid, love that's made her appreciate herself as she never had before. For yourselves and all those who see you that's the sacrament: you, the living symbols of Christ and the Church, whose love is what makes the world go round.

When we deal with God there's always a danger that we won't see the woods for the trees. That was the reason for all the prayers and ceremonies at the wedding. They were reminders.

But that's all they were. Your marriage is a sacrament, but that sacrament is just your work, your joy in each other. That sacrament, that living symbol of Christ and his Church, is simply you.

Like every sacrament it's a holy thing. It will make you holy. The good you'll receive from it won't depend on fate or chance. Marriage will be whatever you make it, and what you make it will depend on what you think you can make it.

If you just look at each other, you'll be afraid. Who wouldn't be? Who can see the future? But if you just look at each other, you'll miss the most important thing that the wedding liturgy was supposed to tell you. Why is your marriage holy? Because it's an invitation from Christ to work in company with him. Why will it make you holy? Because he hasn't just made you husband and wife. That sacrament he conferred on you will change you, make you able to do the things he commissioned you to do, to be the husband and wife you want to be.

One day two of his apostles approached him and asked if they could be his special followers. They wanted to be close to him, always at his side. He looked at them. "Can you drink from the cup I'm drinking from, not looking out for yourselves, giving even your lives for the work I'll entrust to you?"

They knew they were weak but that he'd be with them. They answered, "Yes. We can." He loved them for that. It was what he wanted them to say.

You came arm in arm to the altar one morning to tell him, "We want to be close to you, and we think we can do it better together." By accepting your wedding promises through the priest who represented him, he told you, "You're right. You'll do each other more good than you can dream of. But don't look for visions and ecstasies. You won't be wearing halos. That permanent holy symbol will be simply your work, your joy in each other. The sacrament will be you. Your life together will have the usual ups and downs. It will look as ordinary as mine. Can you drink from the cup I'm drinking from?"

Like those other two followers of his, you knew you were weak. But you also knew that he'd help you. You were right. As a husband and wife you can take his cup at communion time, drink from it and tell him what he wants so much to hear: "Yes. We can." Because you feel so generous and courageous? No. Because you know you've been given what St. Paul used to describe as a "gift."

What kind of gift? Well, Paul says it's a grace, but one that's very different from the usual kind. Like any grace it's a favor that a man receives from God, but this one is not for himself alone. It's an assignment, a commission to a certain rank, a part to play in the history of the Church. It always involves two things: a special job to do for the people of God and special help to do it. Paul himself had been given one of these gifts. So had the apostles. So has a priest. So have a bride and groom. Marriage is a grace that Christ gives to a man and a woman.

And this grace is not for themselves alone.

"Do you see this woman?" he says to the

groom. "I've formed her, made her like no other woman, given her parents to care for her, watched over her myself. But this has only been the beginning. I have so many plans for her, so many blessings that I want to pour out to her. Will you help me? I want to do it through you. This gift I'm about to give you is not for yourself alone. From now on your work in life is to be my love for her."

To the bride he says, "Do you see this man? I've made him. He's my handiwork, my pride. There's so much good I want to do for him, so much happiness I want to bring him. Will you help me? I want to do it through you. This gift I'm about to give you is not for yourself alone. From now on your work in life is to be my love for him."

To the two of them as they stand there at the altar Christ himself says, "Do you see that world out there? Do you see all those people I've made? Do you realize how much they mean to me? Death on a cross was not too high a price for the good I want to bring them. And I want to do it through you. The number of human beings in heaven is going to depend on you. Children are going to learn what goodness is by watching you. People whom you don't even know yet are going to realize how much they mean to me by noticing how much they mean to you. This gift I'm about to give you is not for yourselves alone. From now on your work in life is to be my love for men."

This is why a husband and wife should look at each other with amazement. They've been awarded a gift that's as real and as holy as that of any priest. What scripture says of a priest can be said of them: "No one takes this honor to himself — only those who are called. . . ." Yes; that priest who stood there facing you didn't marry you. He was only a witness. Having him there was just the Lord's way of assuring you that you really were receiving this gift. He's the one who made you husband and wife.

The priest only wasted your time if he told you about the obligations of marriage. You knew them already. For some reason they always feel obliged to remind you that, just like Christ with his vocation, you're going to have your Good Fridays. But this wasn't news to you. What you needed so much to know, and what you need to know even more now that you've seen what it means to be married, is not to be afraid. This enterprise of yours has a silent partner. In fact, the whole thing was his idea, not yours. Marriage is a vocation. You've been called, made for this marriage, made for each other.

Why? Because he wants to make each of you happier than you've ever dreamed of being. He wants to make you better, bring you closer to him than you've ever been before. Your life together is a sacrament, and we're told that the more sacramental life we have, the more completely God is present in us in a temple. So the first gift you gave your wife was Christ. The first good that you brought to your nervous husband was Christ. This is why he wants you to trust him that your love will grow. Two persons joined to him are joined to each other.

*I shall but love thee
better after death.*

E. B. Browning

A Word of Caution

Staying in love is an art. There are things you do and things you don't do. But they aren't the things that make the difference. All they do is help life itself with its three experiences, work, tears or laughs, and God, to have their effect on love. Hearing so much about this art of staying in love shouldn't make a couple think they have to be constantly on edge. They already have the only thing that can actually make love grow.

That's love itself. It grows by the strangest kind of mathematics. The rate doesn't seem to depend on what someone does for you. It's in proportion to what you do for him. We learn to love by loving. It even makes a person attractive as he's never been before. No two human beings are as beautiful to each other as an elderly husband and wife.

This is why there are no experts in love. It's a constant discovery. You thought you were such a veteran, but you've never really known what it's like. You've never really seen this person.

Words soon get in your way. All the two of you need is to be together. There isn't any constant emotion. It's grown too deep for that. You feel less and less, but you need each other more and more. The only constant thing is a wish, "If we could just start over again, knowing what we know now."

Lovers take each other "till death do us part." Then a day comes when they learn the truth of the claim in the *Song of Songs* that "Love is strong as death." The liturgy tells them life is only changed, not taken away. And so is love. St. Paul says it's the one thing we'll take with us. A husband and wife will always have each other. For all time to come they'll be one in Christ.

Love is always patient and kind; it is never jealous; love is never boastful or conceited; it is never rude or selfish; it does not take offense, and is not resentful. Love takes no pleasure in other people's sins but delights in the truth; it is always ready to excuse, to trust, to hope, and to endure whatever comes.

Paul to the Corinthians